Top 9 Rules for Small Business

Top 9 Rules for Small Business

VIOLATE THEM AND IT COULD COST YOU MILLIONS

Derek Bowers

ISBN-13: 9781548463519
ISBN-10: 1548463515

To my parents, Al and Beverly, who taught me to believe that nothing is impossible and everything always works out for the best. And to my wife, Karen, for her faith in me, no matter what adventure I embark upon.

Contents

Acknowledgments ·ix

Introduction: Business Is for Profit ·xi

Rule 1   Master the Gold · 1

Rule 2   Rent Control· 5

Rule 3   Employees Are *Not* Your Friends· 8

Rule 4   Your Banker Is the Enemy · 12

Rule 5   Don't Invest Unless You Get Control· 15

Rule 6   Partnerships and Joint Ventures Usually Don't Work · · · · · · · · · · · · · · · · 17

Rule 7   The Myth about Patents and Trademarks· 19

Rule 8   Incorporate—But Beware · 20

Rule 9   Simple Rules about Selling Your Baby· 21

The Unwritten Rule
PART I: The Boat Analogy · 23

PART II: The Lifeboat Analogy · 34

Acknowledgments

G rowing up, I was blessed with incredible family members, and to this day, they continue to inspire and support each other to no end. My family has grown, and of course, I have added my own wife and children too.

So, I offer a heartfelt thanks to the following:

My siblings, Mark, Deby, and Rennie. You allowed me to watch and learn from your successes and failures all my life. I am forever grateful for the support and encouragement you gave your little brother.

Mark is the amazing graphics wizard who still makes my crazy ideas look professional—including this book, my second publication. Deby is my big sister, who taught me to read before I was in kindergarten and continues to uphold the family traditions that our mom began. Rennie is my lifelong business partner, with whom I have shared a room and a company. Our companies still do business with each other.

My mom, Beverly, was the first entrepreneur of our family. Once I was in school, she and her best friend, Betty, took some oil-painting lessons. This launched her on a successful career as an artist that spanned twenty years. By the end of her life, she had limited-edition lithographs selling in art galleries across the country. Painting never made her rich, but I learned from her about the richness of doing something you are passionate about.

My mom was also my first business consultant and mentor. When I was very young, my brother Rennie and his friends staged elaborate skits and plays in our neighborhood. I got to be an actor, stagehand, and concessionaire. My mom made us calculate the costs of and pay for all of our popcorn, soda, sugar for lemonade, and even each paper cup. This helped us set prices so we could make a profit. By the time I was nine or ten, my mom allowed me to create and sell my own paintings at her art shows. Of course, we calculated the costs of materials.

But my dad, Al, may have been the biggest influence in my life. Once my older siblings were well on their way to independence, he had more time to spend with me. He coached my baseball teams, led our scout troops, and was president of the athletic-booster club at my high school. (I did a lot of activities—but my dad was in more photos in my high-school yearbook than me!)

Car rides with Dad to my youth activities were the most powerful and formative times in my life. We used to playfully debate the premise that "nothing is impossible." As always, he had a logical answer for every one of my questions. We discussed everything from science to philosophy to life situations. Today, I continue this tradition in car rides with my daughter, Danielle, who was a high-level, competitive softball player in her youth and now plays in a top Division I college program.

In my teens, I was able to watch my dad work as a TV salesperson, store manager, and service repairman back when TVs were sold at small specialty shops. When I was in high school, my dad took a leap of faith and started a new career, even though he was nearly fifty. Realizing that TVs were becoming disposable commodities, he became a line technician at a high-tech communications company. While working full-time, he went back to school for his quality-engineering degree. Eventually, he became the manager of both the test and quality departments. We kids never sensed that he had any stress or anxiety during any of this.

My dad is eighty-seven now, and he still has great advice to give, even if it's just a chuckle about something I'm going through that he also has gone through before. I inherited his honesty and easygoing temperament, but mostly, I learned from him that the winner of the game of life is the one who makes a positive impact on others, especially children. I imagine that's probably a big reason that I founded a youth softball organization a few years ago and continue to be very involved in and passionate about youth softball.

In addition to my family, I have had some incredible coaches, mentors, and consultants who inspired me to write this book and share my experiences to help others. Special thanks to Robert Schultz, Frank Marotti, Marian Gault, Cliff Monroe, Steven Nasiri, Chris Wilmoth, Andrew Hogan, Chris Borch, Sheri Benjamin, Dennis Dauenhauer, Henry Kim, and my CPA, Sheila Joyce Kellerman.

INTRODUCTION
Business Is for Profit

I assume that if you're reading this book, you're the owner of a small for-profit company. In other words, you want to make money with your small business. Break the rules I lay out here, and you may risk everything.

Over the thirty-plus years of my career, I have come to a profound conclusion. Businesses survive if they make money. Sure, a few people have gotten rich by having smart ideas that made money quickly and didn't grow businesses around them. But the collapse of the dot-com era in the nineties reminded us that bright ideas are usually not enough.

This is not a marketing, customer-service, or sales-nurturing book. There are hundreds of others for all of that. This book is about the rules for operating a company that aims to grow. It is intended to help small-business owners and managers avoid some of the most costly financial mistakes that I have seen—or made myself. Its rules can apply whether your business is just getting started or you're in the middle of running it. If you've already experienced the cost of violating one of these rules, let this book be a reminder of what not to do. This book is intended to be a quick read that you will, I hope, refer to over and over again.

I founded my first high-tech company when I was twenty-six years old. Starting in a spare bedroom, I transformed it into a multimillion-dollar world leader in semiconductor test accessories. We were listed as one of *Inc.* magazine's Fastest Growing Private Companies in the Country (#105) and as one of *Silicon Valley Business Journal's* Fastest 100 (#35). Eventually, I sold my company.

Over the last thirty years, I have founded multiple start-ups, joint ventures, partnerships, and family-owned companies, and I have worked on both sides of merger and acquisition transactions. I don't list these things to impress you but to give you evidence that I have valuable tips for avoiding financial pitfalls.

Heed my warning: Violating these top 9 rules could cost you millions. Trust me—I know from firsthand experience.

In addition to the top 9 rules, I have also included the secret to the unwritten rule. You will learn that this is as important as the other rules or maybe more.

Read on, learn, and enjoy.

RULE 1

Master the Gold

I f you own a business, it doesn't matter whether your background is in sales, manufacturing, or engineering: you must become an expert in your company's finances.
There is nobody, except you, the owner, who can be trusted to maintain the overall
profitability of your company. It's your pocket that the cash comes out of if things go
wrong. No matter how good your accountant, CFO, or CPA is, each has a different
agenda than owners do.

It's your bank account.

You must be in control of your bank account. How many times have you read news
about a small-business owner losing thousands of dollars due to a trusted employee's
mistake or theft? If your company is large enough that you need to delegate purchase
approvals, set signature levels at certain dollar amounts. Major amounts must require
your signature.

You should also sign all supplier payments. Monitor payroll closely, and never
have the same person collecting the deposits and preparing the checks. If you must
have a petty-cash account, limit it if at all possible (your accountant will love you for
this too).

Cash is king.

Everyone has heard this phrase, and it is really true for a small business. Cash is the life-
blood of your operation. You need cash to be able to evaluate the business's financial

decisions correctly. For example, you could pay cash for a piece of equipment rather than incur additional costly finance fees.

Become a cash hoarder. It can help keep your stress level lower. The most stressful times I have ever had in business were when cash availability was tight. Once you earn some cash, be stingy about letting it go. However, it takes a lot of gross profit to generate spare cash in the bank.

I'll let you and your tax advisor figure out the best way to hoard cash—inside the business and/or outside the business in your personal accounts. *Warning: make sure you follow rule 8!*

Manage receivables.

Your accounts receivable can be a large repository for cash. Mismanagement or neglect of them can ruin your business. One delinquent account can put a huge roadblock in your cash planning. Beware of changes in payment patterns! They can be a sign that your customer is in trouble. Often, it's your best customer that starts to string out payments. There are so many horror stories about companies that are ruined because their largest customer goes bankrupt without notice.

Be consistent with your payment monitoring and notices. If you threaten to charge interest, then do it. You will find out that many times, your late-payment problems go away when it starts to cost customers real money. They will choose to hold back someone else's payments. The caution is to make sure you have positive communication along the way. You don't want to irritate the customer either. It's OK to be flexible with payment terms for key accounts as long as they keep up their end of the bargain.

Manage payroll.

Out-of-control payroll is another common way a company can be destroyed. (We will also address payroll in rule 2 and rule 3, as this is a very important factor in every company.)

Employees celebrate payday, and before you ran a company, you did too. It was a joy that you looked forward to. Now that you are managing the outflow of money, payday can seem like a constant burden.

If you have shift employees, such as in a retail environment, you must train and monitor your managers so that you are never under- or overstaffed—or as close to that ideal as possible. This is a tricky art to master, but the most successful companies invest whatever is necessary to perfect it into a consistent science. Understaffing leads to unhappy customers who leave to patronize your competitors. Overstaffing can easily and quickly drain your cash reserves.

In an industrial environment, think twice before pulling the trigger on a new hire. There are many obvious and also hidden expenses that come with every employee. For example, training costs you not only the new employee's time but also that of the manager who does the training. For a new employee in manufacturing, there also may be excess material costs or scrapping due to the learning curve.

For a flexible workforce, use outsourcing. You can easily stop using such an outside company if business drops. Of course, there are economic considerations to every make-versus-buy decision. You will also need to make sure you don't violate any laws covering the use of independent contractors.

The bottom line is that no matter how many financial managers he or she has, a small-business owner must personally monitor payroll very closely. I will go into more detail about this in rule 3.

Inventory sucks.

Yes, inventory sucks the life out of your business. Inventory is cash on the shelf that you can't use, and you always risk losing it completely. Inventory can get lost, become obsolete, spoil, be stolen, or be destroyed. Business owners must control inventory wisely.

True story: My first business was flying along and growing like crazy. We had nearly fifty employees, and sales were over $7 million that year—nearly 50 percent more than the prior year. On paper, we had great margins and showed a healthy profit, yet we had no cash in the bank. Better late than never...

As the year was winding down, I decided to investigate and started to ask questions. I zeroed in on my vice president of operations, who had been with the company about a year. I had assumed that everything had been running correctly. After all, he had come from a much larger manufacturing company and was presumably an expert. Shipments were getting out the door, so everything had seemed fine. Suddenly, this VP announced his resignation. I think he realized that I had figured out what had been happening.

I found that I had assumed too much and had neglected to monitor our purchasing. My VP had made the mistake of bulk-purchasing items that we had custom designed for a single use only. That meant that we had a bunch of parts on the shelf that we had no use for. Inventory was over $1 million at that time—probably ten times what was required for our business level then. What does this mean in terms of cash? We should have had $1 million in the bank instead of none.

We were able to salvage about half of this inventory by adding labor to modify it for use; the rest was scrapped. The bottom line was a net loss of probably $750,000.

To avoid this problem permanently, we set levels of inventory values with respect to sales, and I monitored the ratio monthly. We also renegotiated with our suppliers to issue bulk purchase orders and yet were able to receive goods monthly or as needed. This plugged one of the major cash leaks.

This was a great example of a rule 1 violation: I had assumed my VP of operations had been managing inventory (cash) correctly.

Protect your gold.

Make sure you have some cash set aside for any legal issues that may come up. Legal challenges never come at a good time, and they can be devastating if you don't have any cash to defend yourself. Many businesses have died due to a single legal problem.

True story: In California, there is a small team of people that files Americans with Disabilities Act (ADA) violation lawsuits against small businesses that do not have facilities properly set up for disabled patrons. They secretly visit public facilities and take photos and measurements. A violation could be a wheelchair ramp at the wrong angle, or, as in one case, having sanitized toilet-seat covers sitting on the tanks rather than hung on the wall at a specified height and distance from toilets. Each violation could cost thousands. Most small businesses are likely to settle such lawsuits with some amount of cash plus make costly repairs.

RULE 2

Rent Control

All businesses start somewhere. At some point, your business may outgrow your home or the building(s) it occupies now. The decisions you make regarding facilities can truly make or break your company. Never rent more space than is absolutely necessary for your business.

Having a prestigious office space can be fun and give you a sense of pride when someone comes to visit. However, this luxury item can be one of the most expensive fixed costs in your business.

There are other costs to business property that are not as obvious. The more space you have, the more office furniture you usually need. Your utilities go up dramatically just to light, heat, and cool a larger office space.

If you are able to lay out your office space, beware of "dead space." Dead space is square footage that does not contribute to your bottom-line profit. Conference rooms, restrooms, break rooms, and even hallways are virtually dead space. You pay rent on that square footage every month. You heat, cool, light, and clean those spaces too. This can translate to a lot of cash lost forever.

There are ways to save on office or manufacturing space. Some are more traditional, and some are more modern and utilize today's technology. Consider these options:

Virtual office. Many home-based businesses establish a professional address with a rented mailbox. They use coffee shops and their customers' offices for business meetings. For large meetings, you could rent a conference room at a hotel or restaurant.

Multiple shifts. Multiple shifts that "reuse" your space at different times can double or triple the output of the square footage and equipment you have. The key to success here is proper training and monitoring of the shift manager. Clear expectations are required every shift to get your desired results.

Work share / work from home. With today's technologies, such as direct Internet access to company files and videoconferencing, many employees can work from home. Your office can be a flexible space where employees come in when needed, and they can share computer stations and such.

Outsource everything. As I've noted, you should outsource anything that is not critical. This not only allows you a flexible labor force to ride the ups and downs of business cycles but also saves a lot of office or manufacturing square footage.

Sublease from a key supplier or partner. This tip can be a win-win for you and a supplier or other partner who has extra space on a temporary or longer-term basis. You may get the space at below-market rates while helping your partner pay for it. You also may improve communication and service between you.

Cubicles versus private offices. In your business, you may need private offices to recruit key managers, but in general, private offices are more expensive and waste square footage compared to cubicles. Keep this in mind as you scout for new business real estate.

True story: I started my first business in my house and then moved to an eight-hundred-square-foot office. Within the first year, we needed to hire more people, so we expanded into the two units on either side. This got us to twenty-one hundred square feet, six offices, and an assembly-lab space.

A few months later, we decided to start our own manufacturing by adding a machine shop. We rented space at our key supplier and hired machinists to work there too. Within a year, we needed to expand manufacturing again and looked for a new building to consolidate everyone's workplaces. We found the perfect space a couple of miles away. It was about seventy-five hundred square feet. One thing we learned was that setting up the machine shop was expensive due to the need for electrical contractors, compressed-air installation, and the drayage to move the shop's heavy machines.

However, business grew consistently year over year. Just within the next year, we grew so much that we had no room for more machines or design engineers. We decided to move again.

Since moving was so expensive, we looked for a building that could handle future expansion so we wouldn't have to move again for a while. We found a building shell and leased twenty-five thousand square feet, working with the landlord to build the walls into the space we wanted. After all was said and done, we had spent more than $250,000 (cash) on new cubicles, electrical, plumbing, alarm systems, phone systems, furniture, and other expenses over and above our landlord's allowance for tenant improvements.

A couple of months before we actually moved in, our industry tanked. Sales dropped by almost 50 percent overnight. We had already spent the money to move, so we figured we would ride out the business down cycle in our new, modern facility. It had been less than three years since I'd moved out of my spare bedroom at home.

I was shocked by how much utility costs skyrocketed in our new building compared to our old place. Signing a rent check for $26,000 a month was not fun either. We were heating and cooling about eleven thousand square feet of unused space.

I realized then the power of outsourcing to ride the cycles of the semiconductor-equipment business. Our growth strategy changed, and we bought no more new equipment for a long time after that. We had plenty of office space for engineering and support personnel, but the eleven thousand of extra square footage was never used.

Unfortunately, the way we had laid out the space did not easily allow for any meaningful sublease of our extra space, so we were stuck with it for the duration of the seven-year lease.

You can easily do the math: eleven thousand square feet multiplied by $1.05 equals $11,550 per month wasted. Seven years of that, plus contracted rent increases, added up to over a million dollars.

We survived the downturn, but that million in rent cash was gone forever. It could have been in our business bank account—or even my own bank account—as a bonus, had we been wiser with our growth strategy.

We did end up re-leasing, but we cut down to fourteen thousand square feet for the next five years.

The lesson here is that we should have expanded into only about ten thousand square feet and then looked for more space if we really needed it. You must control your rent expenses or risk millions of dollars.

RULE 3

Employees Are *Not* Your Friends

Always remember that your employees *work* for you. Absolutely, you want to create a positive work environment, and it's OK to be friendly with them, but you must never allow such relationships to determine business decisions.

Trust me, your loyal and dedicated vice president and best friend can instantly turn into your worst nightmare if he or she perceives some kind of unfair treatment from you. Treat everybody fairly and be consistent.

Employees will never understand what an owner has to deal with. Be careful what information you share with employees. They all have their own agendas and might find a way to use your private or financial information against you.

Establish HR policies and procedures.

Except for joint ventures, my businesses have been mostly located in California. It is one of the most litigious employment environments in the entire United States. Wherever you are, it is imperative that you invest in your human-resource (HR) policies and procedures.

In the United States, it is incredibly easy to start a legal claim against an employer. There are public and private entities ready and willing to assist plaintiffs in their legal pursuits. For the employer, defense can be very costly and time-consuming. For a small business, such expenses can be deadly. Employment-defense lawyers charge hundreds of dollars per hour. Small-business owners are usually the ones who have to spend time away from running their businesses to fight these claims, and even a small claim can cost you thousands or more.

There are many avenues for outsourcing payroll, benefits, and HR functions. Unless you are an expert, I am a big proponent of these services for small businesses. These firms not only help keep you up-to-date with current regulations but also help your bottom line, as outlined in rule 2.

Whatever you do, you must document your policies and follow them. You can't rely on what you tell your employees. Verbal instructions are always open to interpretation. The courts and law offices are full of interpretation cases.

One of the most common and expensive legal actions against employers has to do with wrongful termination. At a minimum, you need clear hiring and firing procedures. There are HR consultants and publications that can help you set these procedures up. Such an investment can have a very high, if not always obvious, financial return.

Treat employees fairly and consistently.

Training and monitoring your managers is the key to fairness in the workplace. It's easy to get lazy and assume that your managers are treating your employees well. You run a small business, so get up and walk around. Talk to employees. More importantly, listen to them. They will tell you how effective your managers are at communication.

Set clear expectations for your managers too. Insanity is letting a manager run a department without any specific guidance and goals but expecting great results. Talk to your managers often—and listen to them too.

There is really no excuse for not knowing what is going on with your employees. The buck stops in your office.

Manage payroll.

I can't stress enough the loss potential of an out-of-control payroll. The business leader who can master this expense is the one who will have the biggest bank account.

Think of every employee as an investment—and if you are a savvy investor, you expect a reasonable return on your investments. You should be getting a profitable return on whatever you pay out every month for an employee. In other words, your employees should each mean more money coming in for the business.

The easy way to measure your return on employees is to see what value each one brings. Your salespeople should be producing sales. For all your manufacturing people, chefs, waiters, or counter clerks, you must have enough customers to support them and make a profit.

The tougher evaluations are of overhead types, like middle managers, human-resources people, and executives. The compensation in these positions should be performance based in some way so that you can adjust to the ups and downs of business. When business is good, they should get rewarded for that. When business is down, everyone must take a hit. The more employees who have an "owner mentality," the better.

Outsource your workers.

There are many ways to outsource a lot of business functions these days. Payroll services, human-resources functions, and bookkeepers can all be contracted on an as-you-need basis. Only when it makes financial sense should you hire a direct employee instead of outsourced help. Direct employees have a lot of costs over and above the office space they take up. You must account for benefits, vacations, sick time, social security, workers' compensation insurance, and general sitting-around, unproductive time.

Another thing you need to become an expert in is deciding when to add someone or just have the existing crew work overtime. One of the most critical factors to consider is the training time it takes to get a new employee up to 100 percent production (and therefore a profitable return on your investment).

Laying off or firing people can be an expensive distraction and a morale killer, as well, but don't be afraid to get rid of someone if your business can't sustain that person profitably. It's usually financially better to cut more swiftly and hire back later as business returns. It's possible for a small business to cut back everybody's pay across the board during tough times, but that can really kill productivity in the long run. Employees sometimes can develop a "you owe me" mentality. And often, it's your most productive employees who leave at these times.

One other thing to watch is the pay of longtime employees. It's common for loyal old-timers to get systematic raises year after year until they are being overpaid. Pay scales must be handled carefully. Firing someone and hiring a lower-cost replacement can get you in hot water with government agencies and the court system.

True story: One of the companies I have consulted with had a relatively expensive manager who had a large number of employees reporting directly to him. Over the years, as the company grew, his salary did too.

There were no problems with the manager's performance, but as the business climate changed, his department became smaller and smaller. Eventually, he was a senior manager of only three people. His salary did not match his job anymore, and there was nowhere else in the company he could transfer. At this point, the company had to make some decisions. The star manager and the company were able to renegotiate his salary and bring it more in line, but he no longer seemed to put as much extra effort into his job. Gone were the days when he'd stay late just to get something done.

I think a better way of handling the situation would have been to renegotiate the nature of his job too. If achievable milestones had been set with corresponding financial rewards for him, the company might have been able to preserve his star performance.

Overall, you must manage the business first when making hiring and firing decisions. Employees are investments, not friends. Confuse the two, and it can cost you millions.

RULE 4

Your Banker Is the Enemy

A ll businesses need banks. But remember the old saying, "Keep your friends close and your enemies closer"? It truly applies to your banker.

Beyond normal services like checking, savings, and wire transfers, there is a tempting service available to growing companies: beware of the seductive credit line.

Growing companies can be cash strapped. While their receivable accounts grow, their checking accounts thin out. Many turn to their banks for credit lines.

A credit line is like an on-demand loan that is easily accessible by either a phone call or Internet transaction; you draw money from the bank to your company up to the amount it has decided you may borrow. These are secured loans, and the collateral for them is often a small company's accounts receivable (AR). That is, the bank is using the amount that a company's customers owe it as a guarantee of repayment on the loan. Most small-business owners must also sign a personal guarantee. This is because a typical small business does not have a lot of tangible assets to guarantee the bank that its money will be repaid with interest. A personal guarantee is when a business owner attaches his or her personal assets to the bank loan. This is very risky because if your business can't pay the loan, the bank can be ruthless in collecting the debt by taking your personal money and property.

Read your loan documents carefully. Be warned that there are strict terms and conditions for the use of this cash! Credit-line agreements come with covenants, or terms of the loan. Along with annual fees and interest, the bank usually requires monthly or quarterly financial statements, which it monitors carefully. Banks have separate divisions that do this work to minimize their risk. For example, if your business AR total falls below a certain amount, or maybe the ratio of what you owe (payables) goes over what the bank wants to see, then you are in violation of the terms of the loan agreement.

Your slow-paying customers are no help either. Banks don't usually count money owed to you for invoices older than sixty or ninety days. They consider that money too risky for collection, so they just eliminate it from your equation. They don't care if the customer has a particular relationship with you; it's not personal. It's just a math formula for them.

And your local banker may have no influence on the loan-enforcement department. That's what happened to me with my first company.

True story: My business was growing fast and making money. Following the advice of my CPA, we opened a credit line. I had always heard that you should establish a credit line when you don't need it. It's true; banks love companies like that—because wealthy companies still pay the banks an annual fee even if they never draw money from their credit lines. My bank was no exception. I had a great rapport with the branch manager too.

When we had a semiconductor downturn, we decided to try to hunker down and weather the storm. That meant that even though sales dropped by 30 percent for a couple of months, we figured it was better to keep all of our employees so we would be ready for the next upturn. We drew cash on our credit line for payroll.

This went on for a few months. One month, it looked like things were coming back, but then the next month would be slow again. We cut our spending wherever we could but still drew more and more cash from the bank.

Then, it happened without warning: One day at the office, we received registered letters from our bank—three, in fact. One was addressed to our corporation, one to me, and one to my vice president and business partner. Not only that, the bank sent registered letters to our homes regarding our personal assets.

These letters stated that due to our current financials, our company was not in compliance with the terms of the loan and we had thirty days to repay the entire $362,000 or face legal collections action, both corporate and personal, since we had signed personal guarantees. Again, this was without warning.

I had assumed we had a great relationship with the bank and that the bankers were our friends and business partners. I had assumed that eventually, the economy would turn around, and then we would repay the loan. Sure, we paid interest, but that seemed fair. I was wrong.

Well, we did not have anywhere near that type of cash available in the company. If we had, we wouldn't have used the credit line. It would also have been a difficult burden to get it personally. I was filled with frustration, shock, anxiety, and stress.

I called my bank's branch manager. She told me that the collections department had specifically instructed her not to warn us. I assumed that this was their way of making sure they were in control and that the company in question would have no time to try to hide money and so on. It was also an intimidation tactic, and it worked very well.

Then my wife called me. After I explained and calmed her down, I got a call from my business partner's wife. That was not fun either. As president and founder, I had to resolve the issue. If the bank had intended to get my attention, well, it did. That was a dark and lonely day at the top.

After a couple of days of scrambling, pleading with the bank's collections department, and getting some help from my branch manager and advice from our CPA, we finally all agreed on a detailed ninety-day payback plan.

We were able to get some tax breaks due to the poor economy. We also restructured payments to some vendors and got some help from our largest customer via some old invoices that they finally settled. We also made some overdue payroll cuts—letting these ride was a serious rule 3 violation.

We made the deadline to pay off the credit line. The next month, we changed banks. And we never opened a credit line again.

The debacle proved that our banker was not really our friend. Our banker actually became the enemy. So remember the saying about friends and enemies. Work with your bankers and use their help, but be cautious.

And avoid personal guarantees. The bank is not afraid to call them when due.

If you do borrow money, make sure you follow all of the other rules in this book. Credit lines and loans may help when the business is growing, but it's not wise to use them when the economy is going the other way.

RULE 5

Don't Invest Unless You Get Control

At some point, almost all successful company owners are approached by friends, relatives, or acquaintances who ask them to invest in some kind of side business venture. It could be related to your current business or something completely different.

For example, a restaurant owner might be asked to become a partner in another type of restaurant. A construction contractor might be offered a stake in a real-estate development. Maybe a retail-shop owner might get an opportunity to invest in the next big Internet venture.

Whatever the opportunity is, you must beware of the real risks involved in these types of "outside" investments. Realize that there is a reason that your business has been successful. That reason is you. *You* have been the one controlling the business decisions.

Whenever you are a minority partner, you are at the mercy of the majority partner to make a return on your investment. I have known so many folks who have lost everything in cases like these.

True story: One of my joint ventures was to enter a parallel market to my main company. On the surface, it looked like a great opportunity. We would design and manufacture everything for this new company, but it would manage the sales and business functions. The founder was a seasoned sales executive with years of experience in this market. We assumed it would be a great success.

However, our expertise was in relating to and working closely with the customers during development. That way, we knew what the customer's challenges were and could address them directly. But here, our joint venture (JV) was managed by this other guy. We kept building part after part, trying to break into this market. All the time, he kept finding new customers to try our product.

We had dedicated a full-time designer and had to use our best machinists to try to get these products developed. In the end, the technology that was the basis for the product was not suitable for the application. After sinking in about six months and $250,000, we dissolved the joint venture and just absorbed those expenses. We were so busy with our core business that we didn't have time to chase after any losses.

The lesson we learned is that had we been in direct contact with the customer, we would likely have discovered the fundamental challenge of the technology sooner. Being an engineering-based company, we might have been able to find a different technology to service that market instead of riding the other technology out. In fact, our old business partner ended up joining another company in sales and helped build a successful business using a different technology in that same market.

Another example that can violate rule 5 is using independent sales representatives. Sales reps, by nature, want to open the doors for new customers and then just collect royalties on your ongoing sales. Depending on your product or service, this may or may not work. If you are a customer-service driven organization, sales reps get pushed out of the way as soon as the first quotation is issued to the customer. Typically, your staff works closely with the customer from then on, and the sales rep will continue to get paid without doing much work.

My experience is that to successfully manage independent sales reps, you must have a sales manager, your employee, on the road constantly to make sure they are representing your product well. The bottom line is that since the rep company is not under your control, reps go wherever the easiest money is available. This means that you might not be their top priority, and therefore you may not get the sales production you want. Pick the wrong partner, and you risk negative representation. The upside is that it usually doesn't cost you any cash if a rep doesn't produce. Sales reps may also help establish new regions while you build up enough sales to justify dedicating someone to directly service those regions.

RULE 6

Partnerships and Joint Ventures Usually Don't Work

n my opinion, the worst business you can get involved with is a fifty-fifty type of partnership. To be healthy, the business needs a leader who has ultimate decision power. (Rule 5 applies here too.) If the final decision power is divided equally, it can spell the end of friendships, marriages, and other relationships. No matter how similar the ideas and goals of two partners are at the beginning, over time, the business will change—and so will the partners.

Working in a small business with any active partners can be a recipe for drama. Often, conflicts arise when one partner believes that he or she is putting in more work than another partner (no matter how the percentage of ownership is split up).

My opinion is that you should also avoid partnerships with family members. I suggest that you don't mix money with family. You want your family relationships to flourish, and you will need family members for emotional support during tough business times. Some people are able to work with their family members in business relationships, but that is rare.

If you hire a family member, remember rule 3: employees are not your friends. Disciplining or firing a family member can destroy multiple relationships as the drama unfolds.

JVs are different, but they also have major challenges. JVs are usually formed when two companies' strengths complement each other in a way that seems mutually beneficial. It may be two technologies coming together, or maybe one company has strong operations in a certain country or region, the access to which can benefit another company.

The challenge with JVs is to figure how much each partner contributes in relation to how much is taken as a return on investment. Is there enough profit for two companies to share? In order to share technology, key people from each company will need to dedicate their time to getting the new venture going. Can either partner afford to lose the service of those key people in their core businesses?

True story: My first company tried a JV with an overseas-based company. The idea was to use the company's Asian presence to help us compete by selling and producing our products directly in that region. The other company had a fantastic reputation for design and manufacturing and a top management team.

After months of travel and training expenses, we figured out that the market was much more competitive than we had anticipated. In other words, even though the margins were good, they were not good enough for two profit-driven companies to share and feel good about it. The resources required to get the JV going were also too taxing on us, and it affected our core business. We explored a total merger between our two companies, but in the end, we could not agree on terms. We dissolved the JV and had a friendly parting.

RULE 7

The Myth about Patents and Trademarks

The myth of a patent is that it will protect you from competitors that copy your design or technology. What I have found out is that a patent for a small business may not be worth the effort and expense. What I mean by that is that unless you have the resources and time to defend your patent, at most, a patent can give you the right against a larger company bullying you if you didn't have a patent and that company had one. A patent does keep honest people from violating the patent—but not dishonest ones. The example below explains this situation in more detail.

True story: Back in the 1990s, my attorney told me that it would likely cost $250,000 and months of my time to defend our patent against a competitor. He asked me how much business I was losing to the violating company. In the end, it just wasn't worth my time or the cash to fight it. We decided that the best plan of action was to expand effort outdoing our competitor in service.

So that's the decision. Is your patent worth the time, effort, and cost to defend? If the potential of your patent is worth millions, make sure you get a competent patent attorney to ensure strong protection.

Trademarks are similar, except that the cost and effort of getting a trademark is much lower than for patents. Therefore, the expense of getting a trademark may be easier to justify.

Just know that if you have a good idea, someone will copy it. Often, copycats may naively think they are not violating any patents. Be prepared and realize that just because you have a patent or a trademark, it doesn't mean you're in for smooth sailing.

RULE 8

Incorporate—But Beware

I absolutely suggest that you incorporate your small business. The main purpose of incorporating is to give your personal assets some protection if your corporation becomes liable in legal proceedings.

I will leave it to you and your accounting professional to decide what type of corporation you should set up. The tax benefits differ for an S corporation versus a C corporation or even a nonprofit organization.

The main thing to remember is that to maintain your corporate liability protection, you must not commingle your personal finances with the corporation's finances. This is called "piercing the corporate veil." Violate this rule, and you risk your personal assets.

This means you must treat the corporation as an entirely separate entity. Any expenses that the corporation incurs must not be personal expenses. Personal travel, meals, entertainment, home improvements, and vehicles must be handled outside the corporation with your personal funds.

If it is proved in court that your corporate expenses are linked to personal expenses, the court may rule that there really is no separation between the corporate assets and your personal assets.

Of course, there are ways to mix business with pleasure, but you need to document clearly how those expenses are paid. There are ways to properly get cash into and out of your corporation. Again, consult your tax professional on these subjects.

True story: I currently have a corporation where I am the only employee. I have a corporate credit card that I use only for business expenses. I have a payroll service that I use to pay myself and withhold taxes. It's not difficult to manage. It just takes a little discipline.

RULE 9

Simple Rules about Selling Your Baby

I f you decide, for whatever reason, to sell your small business, you are in for an emotional ride.

Selling your business takes the emotional maturity that your "baby" is a business entity and that it's not personal. The first time I sat in a room with prospective buyers for my first business, they told me, "Frankly, your company is worth less than nothing. You would have to pay us to acquire you." After fifteen years of growth, we were worth *less than nothing*? How could that be? Well, you see, even though we had millions in sales, we had a small operating loss. Our products were more those of a service type of business and not those of a high-value, intellectual-property type of business. That buyer was looking at calculating our net worth by multiplying our earnings (profit) over a certain future period of time. Since we had negative profit (loss), multiplying that over the next few years calculated a negative net value for our company. Mildly embarrassed, we walked away. We fixed the profit problem and sold a couple of years later.

How much should you sell your business for? That's a great question. It all depends on how much someone is willing to pay for it. If you have no idea what to ask, it might be worth hiring a business broker. Ask for references and follow up on them before choosing a broker. A business broker can be expensive, but hopefully it can pay you back by getting you a larger sale price.

Many deals done for small businesses involve an "earn-out." That is, some portion of the payment is agreed to be paid out after the close of the sale, and that portion is based on the performance of the business. My caution to you is that you must structure your earn-out in such a way that you have total control of the factors that earn your money. Once a new owner is in charge, it can affect your process of earning unless it's clearly spelled out. (Rule 5 again.) My attorney warned me to consider that most earn-outs turn out to be zero. Unfortunately, he was correct.

Parent-company stock can also be part of your purchase deal. This means that you get stock in the company that now owns your business. The theory is that owning a small percentage of a much larger entity should be worth more than owning 100 percent of a small entity. However, unless the parent company's stock is publicly traded, there is a huge risk that you never realize a dollar from it. The majority shareholders have all the power.

True story: A large part of the deal for my first company came in the form of shares in the new company, as we were acquired by a larger firm. Immediately after the deal, my shares of the parent company might have been worth 10 to 15 percent of the entire entity. As the new company then acquired other firms, they issued more shares of stock to the investment bankers in exchange for cash to do the acquisitions. This diluted my percentage of ownership. Again, the theory was that a smaller percentage of a much larger company was still worth more in the long run.

Fast-forward to one large acquisition that didn't turn out so well. The company issued more shares to get more cash to operate the business during an economic downturn, and my shares continued to dwindle. The last straw came when the company issued something like a billion shares to get a small amount of cash. This made the value of my stock in the company virtually worthless. These events all happened over about four years.

Bottom line: I recommend that you sell for cash whenever possible. It may require a discount, but at least you know what you're getting.

Make sure you have a good attorney to review your sales deal.

THE UNWRITTEN RULE

PART I: The Boat Analogy

You didn't dream of your business just to be in business. Nobody does. Surprise! There's more to it than all the money you make, as well. There is some driving emotional need that you believed having your business would satisfy. Maybe it was the need to be your own boss or never worry about money again or have freedom over your schedule. Whatever your dream was, I have so far only armed you with nine rules to help you keep the money your business earns. How can you use that resource to stay on track and leverage everything to make your dream a reality? How can you maintain the discipline to follow the nine rules? Good news: there's the most important unwritten rule too.

The unwritten rule is that you didn't get where you are today by accident. Whether you realize it or not, you achieve sustained success in business by following the same basic steps: set a goal, make a plan, execute the plan, and reach the goal. Let's explore how to conscientiously use this rule in everyday business (and in life). Master the unwritten rule, and you will have a lot more money to apply the other nine rules to help keep your money and also enjoy the incredible journey.

Let's imagine that you are the captain of a boat and have a destination you want to reach. You're going from New York Harbor to Antwerp, Belgium, because there is a load of diamonds waiting for you there. Of course, you take out your charts, set a course for Belgium, and sail along your course until you reach your destination.

The business boat.

As the captain of your "business boat," you will define its vision or goal and then chart a course to reach that goal. Often, this chart is called a business plan.

Imagine that your business is a sleek rowboat—the fastest in the world. You have the best rowing athletes manning the oars. You, as captain, are at the helm with your eyes clearly focused on your goal. The diagram below illustrates the team of rowers that works with you to propel you toward the goal. Imagine that your business boat looks like the one in the following diagram.

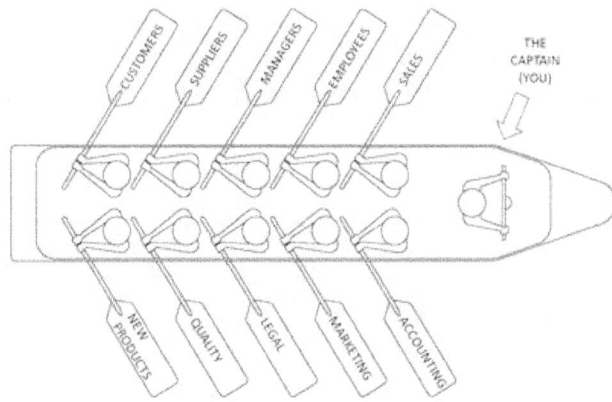

The best-performing businesses have all of their oars synchronized and the rowers rowing in the correct direction at full speed. The captain keeps the boat on course by constantly checking the boat's progress and making adjustments.

In reality, most captains have trouble balancing the rowing team for a number of legitimate reasons. Below, I outline a few different types of captains. Which type are you?

The visionary captain.

Visionary captains are big dreamers. They are so caught up in their vision that they have a hard time dealing with the day-to-day challenges that confront a business. They lose patience with staff members who question their vision or just can't see what they see. Visionary captains dream of a perfect boat without humans that runs at full speed in whatever direction they point it.

The reality is that businesses do have humans. These humans often get frustrated with the visionary captain because they feel that he or she does not listen to them regarding the real challenges they have in trying to follow the dreams. Progress is replaced with dysfunction when communication falls apart. The result is that some departments slow their rowing or, worse, stop rowing at all. How difficult is it to keep your boat on course if your boat is powered like the one in the next diagram?

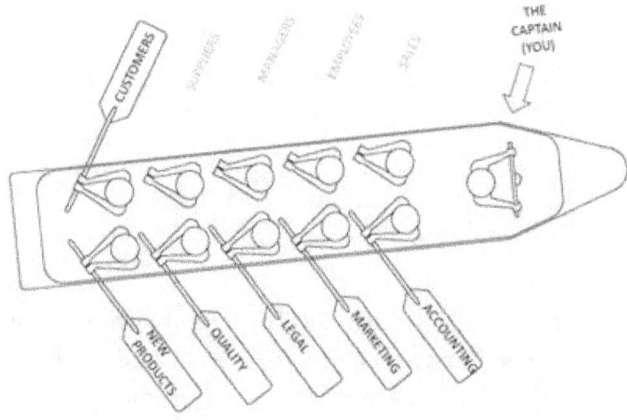

The missing oars on one side mean that the boat constantly veers off course. The business has lost its balance.

The captain-captain.

Captain-captains spend most of their time enjoying the sun on their faces and the wind in their hair. Their life goal was to become a captain. They are happy just being on the sea. They really don't have a big vision, and they lose their grip on the wheel. They also don't have much of a plan. They just handle whatever details of business come their way every day. The captain-captain's boat looks like the next diagram.

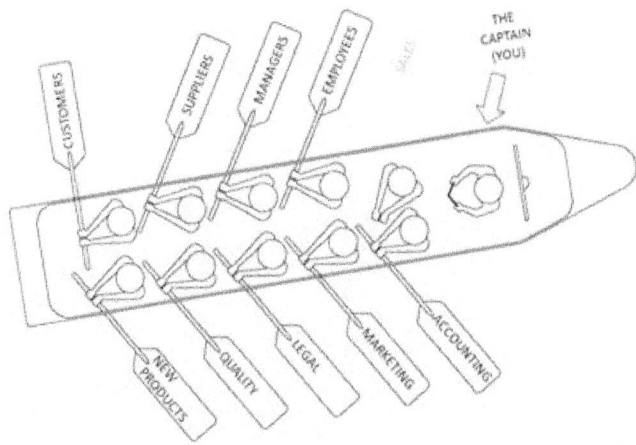

The challenge here is that the boat has no direction. The oars row smoothly and the boat moves, but it wanders all over the sea. Crew members don't feel inspired to go any particular place, but they keep rowing...and not at full speed. It's just a job to them. Top crew members eventually jump ship for a more dynamic boat to row in.

We all know companies with captains like this.

The technician captain.

The technician captain has a real passion for one or more parts of the business. Here, let's imagine that the captain has a very strong background in accounting and loves the numbers. He or she spends so much time and energy on the accounting crew that the other crew members feel disconnected or, worse, row according to their own plans.

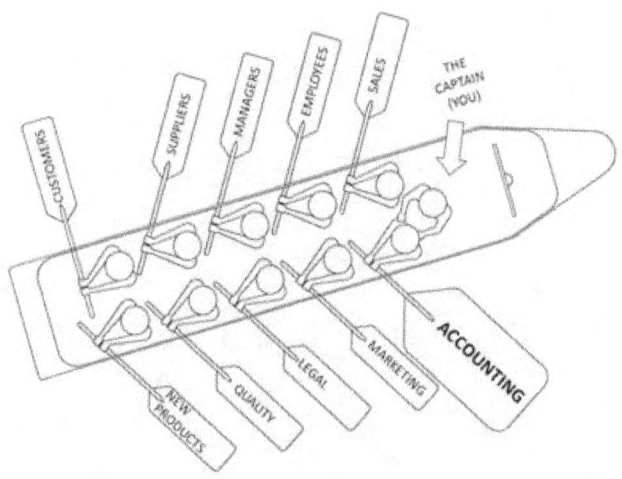

In this boat, the rowing is unbalanced due to the overdeveloped accounting crew, and the others are not rowing efficiently. The captain also tends to lose sight of the overall vision because he or she is focused on only one of the oars.

This boat is often off track.

The micromanaging captain.

The micromanaging captain, instead of focusing on a single task like the technician captain does, scurries up and down the boat and puts his or her hands on every oar.

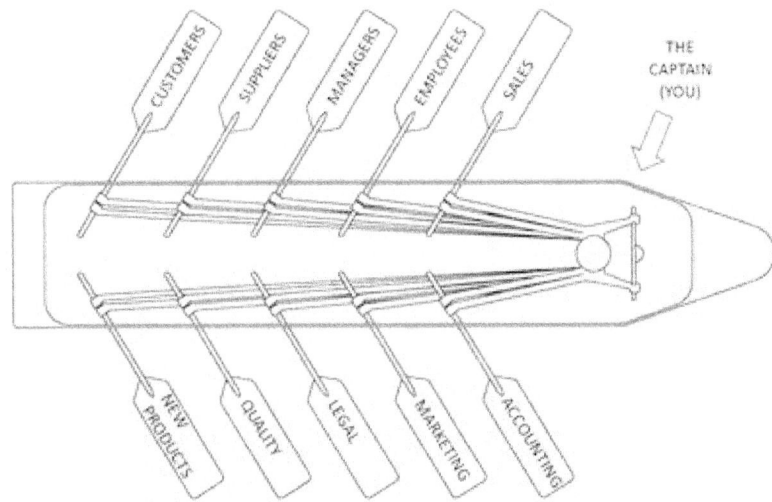

Eventually, the crew members stop rowing because they know that the captain will be there soon to row for them. They also believe that if they start rowing, the micromanaging captain will come and change their course anyway—another reason not to row. Eventually, these rowers feel distrusted and will jump ship just to escape the constant meddling of the captain.

This boat moves in the water but tops out at a very slow speed. Other boats easily pass it.

The ghost captain.

Ghost captains look like they are at the wheel, but they aren't really there. For some reason, they have lost the passion to steer the boat and have mentally checked out.

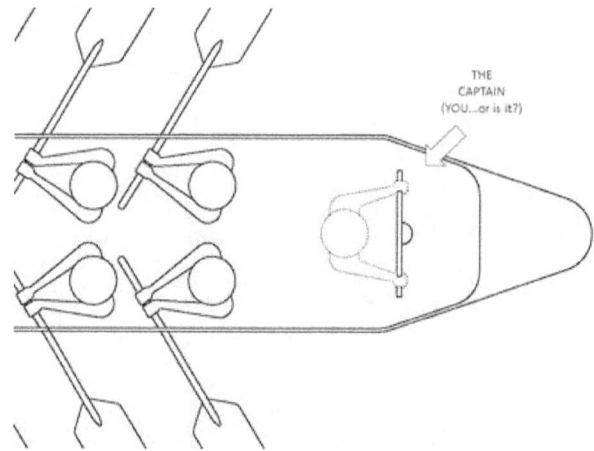

THE
CAPTAIN
(YOU...or is it?)

The reasons that ghost captains become lost can be many. They may have personal issues back on shore that are taking priority.

Maybe they are ghost-visionary captains who are just so frustrated and tired of fighting their crew members that they have checked out and are looking for a new boat to lead.

Maybe they are ghost-captain-captain types who just realized that it's just a job to them too. They realize that they are going nowhere and long for new and exciting adventures. Their thoughts drift away from their boats, and the crew nearly stops rowing altogether.

The ghost-technician captain reminisces about the good old days when he or she was just a top crew member rowing in a fast boat. Life was good. He or she had challenges, and becoming captain someday was a goal to look forward to achieving.

Ghost-micromanaging captains are exhausted. The only reason you even see them at the wheel is that it was the only seat open. They are probably just sleeping.

Mutiny is not the answer.

The solution to these problems is *not* a new captain. The captain simply needs a navigator.

A good navigator has no stake in steering and also has no desire to row the boat. His or her job is to compare the boat's current course with its ideal one and to advise the captain when the boat is adrift.

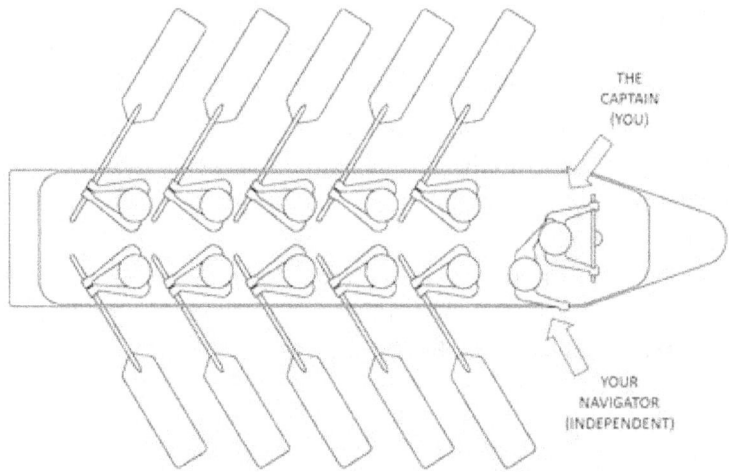

A good navigator makes sure that the captain has accurately defined the course and that the destination is clear. The navigator has a good rapport with the captain and can sense when distractions are a threat. The navigator and the captain meet regularly so that if the boat does drift off course, the navigator can coach the captain to correct the course before a disaster happens. A good navigator can prevent the captain from becoming a ghost—and even bring a ghost captain back to the realm of the living. A good navigator is one of the best investments a captain can make.

The business navigator.

For many successful companies, the navigator role is played by the owner's business coach. A business coach's sole job is to assist the owner.

Unless you are or have been the owner of a company, you cannot understand what stresses an owner must handle. In response to stress, owners tend to become micromanagers, technicians, or even ghosts from time to time. This is natural and common, but the challenge is that the business suffers when it happens. Used properly, a good business coach can reduce or eliminate the frequency and duration of the owner's trips into these mental states.

Are you ready to be coached?

If you are not ready to be coached, do not waste your time and money on hiring a coach. An owner who is not ready is likely to act similarly to the types of captains I've outlined.

I can't tell you how many captain-captain type owners I have talked with. Many of these people "know everything" already and aren't shy about telling you that. They may even be financially secure—but they are leaving money on the table by being totally committed to their captain-captain positions.

If you are still reading this chapter, though, there is some part of you that is ready to learn. It might be worth trying out a coach or two to see if you can achieve some business breakthroughs.

I wrote this book for owners who want more than they have now. They understand that top performers—including professional athletes earning millions of dollars at the top of their game—use coaches. Why not you?

Can you afford a coach?

If you see the value of a business coach, you must find a way to afford one. The value and return on your investment will far outweigh the time and cash you spend. Be sure to measure your return on your coaching investment by keeping an eye on your progress.

How do you find a good coach?

Surprisingly, you may actually already have some coaches in your life. They may be parents, siblings, friends, or other types of mentors. These are the people you turn to for advice. It's good to have many coaches in your life.

True story: My daughter was a high-school student and a college-prospect softball player. Besides her parents, guidance counselor, siblings, and friends, she had her high-school coach, a pitching coach, a hitting coach, and her travel-team coaches. All her coaches challenged her to be better, and they held her accountable. Each one has a unique perspective on a part of her life. So far, the coaching is working very well, and she is now a Division I player in college on a scholarship.

So look to your current circle, and notice your existing coaches. Work to cultivate those relationships even more. They are very valuable—yet some have some limitations.

The limitations are that parents, siblings, friends, and mentors all have stakes in their relationships with you. Emotions come into play, and for fear of damaging a relationship, these coaches may not want to be honest about what they really notice or may not want to hold you accountable. So they can only take you so far. They can even hold you back. For example, I was my daughter's softball coach for years. However, her softball skills and success really went to the next level in her sophomore year, when I stepped aside and focused more on being a parent and let the professional specialists handle the sports side of things.

Similarly, you need an independent business coach. You just need to find one who is the right fit.

Some of the best business coaches don't advertise and work exclusively on referrals, so you could ask a role model whom he or she uses. I have found that most successful people also do not broadcast the fact that they use coaches; they may prefer to keep such a "secret weapon" secret and don't want their competition to catch on. Or relying on a coach can just be an uncomfortable subject that they are afraid people won't understand.

Search the Internet for local coaching and consulting firms. Ask for references, and actually contact them. Test any coach out with a trial period before you sign a long-term contract. Coaches and owners are all different, so what works for one owner may not work for you.

Don't give up. A good coach is worth his or her weight in gold.

PART II: The Lifeboat Analogy

We often discuss business as if it should be our sole focus, but your business should only be part of your life. For owners, it's a very significant part. We imagine that our "lifeboats" look like this:

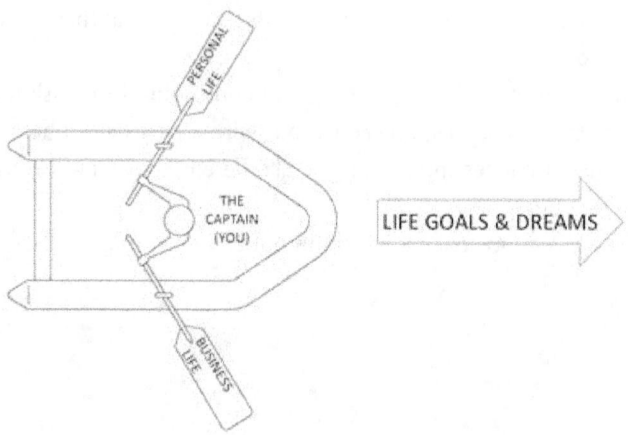

Notice that you, the owner, need your personal-life and business-life oars to row evenly so that you can reach your goals and dreams. All of the extra money you are getting following the nine rules and being successful in business will neither complete your life dreams nor satisfy all of the emotional needs you set out to meet. You must balance your personal lifeboat, as well.

Your personal lifeboat.

Just as we discussed earlier, if one part of your life is too dominant, your boat will just travel in circles. If you neglect your personal life for business success, it will be difficult to reach your overall goals. The same holds true if you neglect your business to handle a personal crisis.

Your personal lifeboat may look like this:

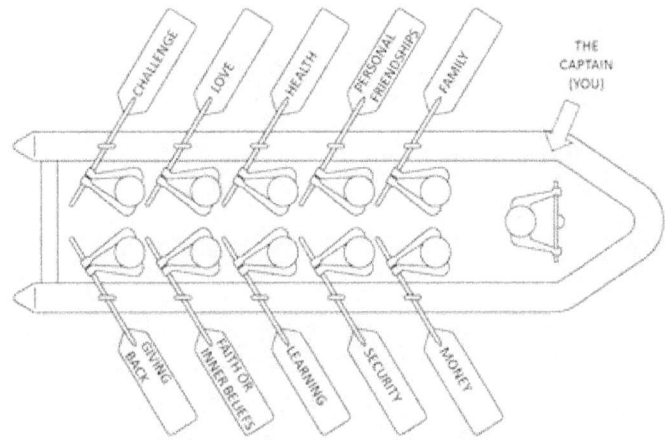

What kind of lifeboat captain are you? Do you expend most of your effort on the easy parts? Maybe you have great friendships but neglect your family or your spouse.

What happens if your personal life and your business life are not aligned? What if you neglect one or the other? Your lifeboat would drift seriously off course.

The bottom line is that you also need a navigator or a coach for your life. If you set things up correctly, your business coach can also help you navigate your life. This fact again illustrates why a family member or a friend does not work as well as an independent coach.

A coach who can help you navigate and balance your business and personal lives is what I call a true executive coach (EC). You are the CEO of your life and deserve a good navigator. Correctly aligning your business and personal power along a defined path toward your life goals is illustrated in the boat below:

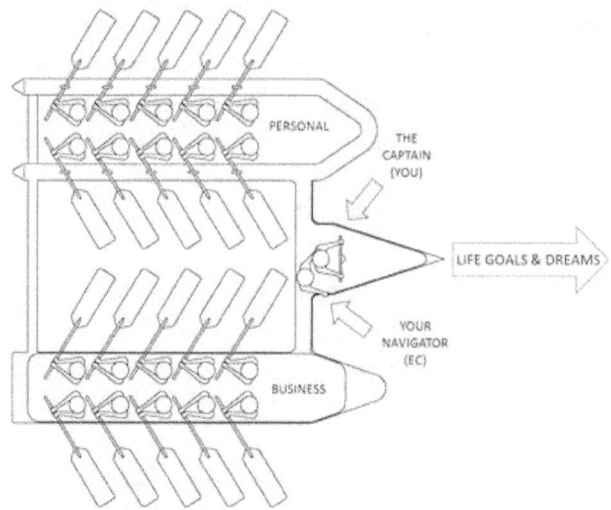

The best EC is fearless about challenging you on every level. For your part, you trust that your EC will handle your challenges with complete discretion, and your EC may be one of the only people in your life with whom you share everything. The power developed in effective EC relationships is beyond the scope of any book. Imagine what you could do with your life if you had clearly defined goals, a plan, and this type of power. What could you accomplish in a year? In two years? Or in a decade? The more defined and the more aligned your personal life and business life are, the easier it is to make decisions to keep you on course.

You now have nine simple rules to help keep your money, plus the bonus of learning the power of leveraging the unwritten rule to keep your life moving swiftly toward your goals. All of the dreams you had when you wanted to start your own business can be real. You can have an abundance of loving relationships, tremendous financial security, ultimate control of your time, and real fun, happily achieving and living an exceptional life.

Get moving, Captain!

Need a business navigator?

Derek Bowers is available for private executive coaching, group training, and business consulting. For more information visit his company's website: X2strategies.com.

www.ingramcontent.com/pod-product-compliance
Lightning Source LLC
Chambersburg PA
CBHW051256170526
45165CB00004B/1732